The author and publishers wish to thank Dr Jane Mainwaring of The Natural History Museum for her help in the preparation of this title.
We have attempted to make the drawings as accurate as possible, but in order to show very small animals clearly the scale may vary in the same picture.

Text © 1992 Judy Allen
Illustrations © 1992 Marianne Birkby
This edition published
in 1996 by Leopard Books,
a division of Random House UK Ltd,
20 Vauxhall Bridge Road,
London SW1V 2SA

First published in 1992 by Julia MacRae Books

All rights reserved. No part of this publication
may be reproduced in any form or by any
means without permission.

ISBN 0 7529 0184 2

Printed in Singapore

WILDLIFE IN THE COUNTRY

· JUDY ALLEN ·

· MARIANNE BIRKBY ·

LEOPARD

Contents

- 6 Farmland
- 8 Hedgerow
- 10 Meadow and Heath
- 12 Moor and Mountain
- 14 Evergreen Wood
- 16 Forest and Wood
- 18 Marsh, Pond and Stream
- 20 Lake and River
- 22 Seashore
- 24 Sea Cliff and Island
- 26 Rare and Endangered Species
- 28 Tree and Plant Spotter's Guide
- 30 Animal and Bird Spotter's Guide
- 32 Glossary

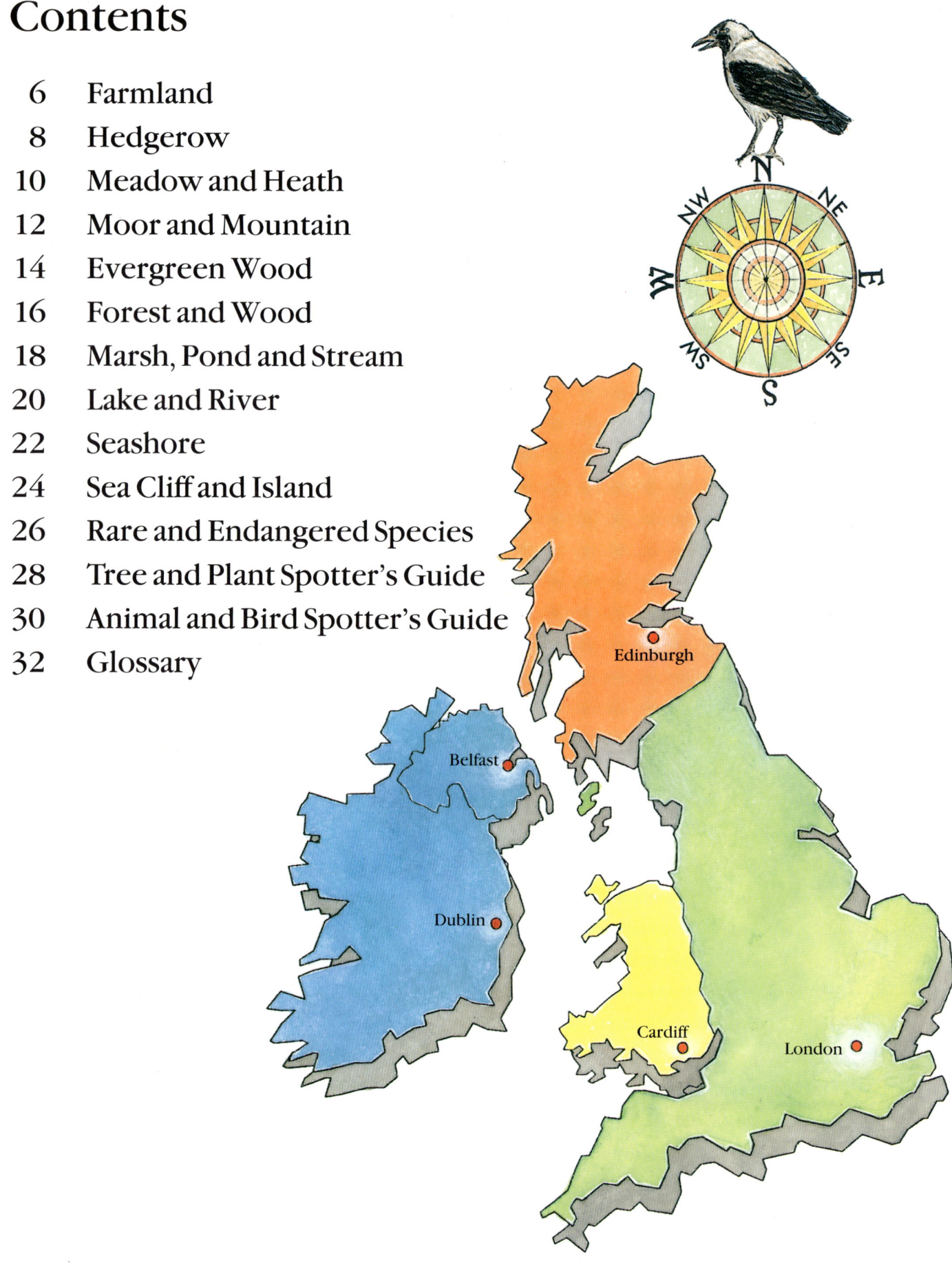

Wildlife in the Country

A walk in the country is more fun when you can recognise some of the trees, plants or animals that you see.

This book takes a look at ten different habitats – from farmland through moors and woods to the seaside – and at the wildlife most likely to be found in each. However, it's useful to know that some things, birds especially, can be found in more than one habitat. For example, the lapwing, which is on the farmland page, can also be seen in meadows and on moorland.

At the end of the book you will find some Spotter's Guides which will give you a bit of extra help recognising the plants and animals you see.

Taking Care

When you explore the country, always have a responsible adult with you. Remember that wild creatures can bite or sting, and berries and toadstools can be poisonous. Ponds, rivers and lakes are often much deeper than you think (never walk out onto ice, however strong it looks) and it is possible to sink in a marsh.

At the seaside, keep back from cliff edges, which can crumble under your feet. If you are walking on the shore, remember that seaweed-covered rocks are slippery. Never go anywhere where you could be cut off by the incoming tide, and take special care near headlands where there are always very strong currents.

Think about the safety of the wildlife, too. Never chase or frighten wild animals and don't steal birds' eggs or pick wild flowers. Although it's fine to collect empty seashells, it isn't fair, and often isn't legal, to take living animals home as pets.

Farmland

BLACK-HEADED GULLS

LAPWINGS

BARN OWL

RABBITS

COUCH GRASS

WOOD PIGEON

MAGPIE

SHREW

SHEPHERD'S PURSE

Wild plants must be tough to grow on farmland where they are attacked with weed killers, or ploughed up, or destroyed when stubble is burned. The roots of couch grass travel underground so the plant can pop up almost anywhere. The sticky seeds of shepherd's purse cling to anything that moves and so are carried to different places. Poppy and wild mustard seeds can lie hidden for years and then sprout when disturbed.

Wood pigeons are pests because they eat most crops. Other birds are welcome. Black-headed gulls and lapwings follow the plough and pick up wireworms and leather-jackets, which eat the roots of new plants. (The wireworm is the larva of the click beetle, the leather-jacket is the larva of the cranefly.) Barn owls, which sleep by day and hunt at night, are encouraged because they feed on harvest mice and shrews. The fox, though, is a mixed blessing – it eats mice, shrews and rabbits, but also pheasants and chickens.

Hedgerow

Some hedgerows are all that is left of an ancient wood, others were deliberately planted to mark boundaries or enclose fields. Many modern farmers have decided hedges take up too much space and have replaced them with wire fences which leave more room for crops. This is sad because an undisturbed hedgerow offers shelter, protection and food to most woodland animals, especially small birds. In fact, a hedge probably has a richer population of wildlife to the square metre than any other area of countryside.

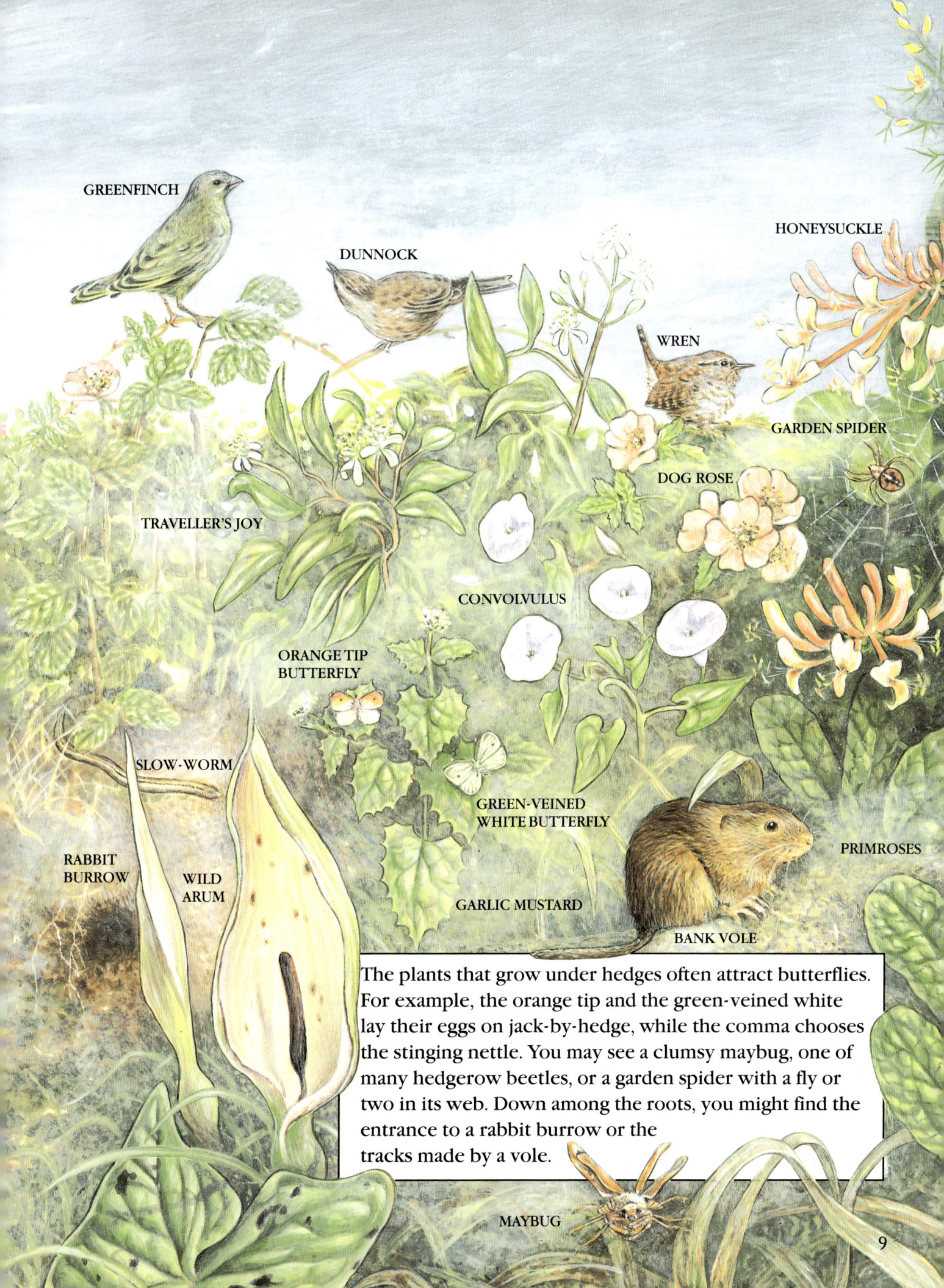

The plants that grow under hedges often attract butterflies. For example, the orange tip and the green-veined white lay their eggs on jack-by-hedge, while the comma chooses the stinging nettle. You may see a clumsy maybug, one of many hedgerow beetles, or a garden spider with a fly or two in its web. Down among the roots, you might find the entrance to a rabbit burrow or the tracks made by a vole.

Meadows have rich soil on which a variety of plants can flourish. The more flowers there are, the more butterflies and other insects there will be. There may even be a crab spider, coloured to match the flower it hunts on.

Birds and other creatures can live in several different places. You can recognise the wheatear, a summer visitor, because it shows white on its rump when it flies. Stoats and weasels look similar to each other, but remember the stoat is bigger and has a black tail-tip. Rabbits are easy to see almost everywhere.

The adder is the only poisonous snake in Britain. It won't harm you if you leave it alone.

Moor and Mountain

The moors and mountains can be bleak and windswept places, and the creatures that live there need to be hardy. This is just as true of the hill farmers' sheep as it is of the wild red deer, the mountain hare and the pygmy shrew. There are few trees, and plants grow close to the ground to shelter from the harsh winds. Among the toughest are the heathers, and the lings which provide food for the red grouse.

The white tufts of cotton grass and the bright green of sphagnum moss can be a useful warning of a blanket bog. Water drains from these high bogs down into the lowlands, forming streams, and eventually rivers.

It is easy to see the merlin when it is hunting, but hard to spot the well-camouflaged curlew which lays its eggs in the moorland grass. You will only glimpse the wildcat if you are in the north of Scotland.

Evergreen Wood

SITKA SPRUCE

CROSSBILL

LONG-EARED OWL

BLACK GROUSE

LESSER REDPOLL

BRACKEN

VOLE

Evergreens are trees that keep their leaves all year round. Many evergreens are conifers, trees with cones. Large plantations of sitka spruce are common – the trees are felled for fence posts, boxes and paper-pulp. Little sunlight reaches the floor of a conifer forest, so not much grows and few creatures live there. The black grouse eats conifer shoots, and the lesser redpoll and the crossbill pick the seeds out of cones. Field voles eat the grass at the plantation's edge – and are hunted by the long-eared owl, which also eats small birds.

When the woodland has a mixture of trees, with scots pine and larch among others, you may, if you are lucky, see roe deer browsing on the saplings and the rare red squirrel feeding in a larch tree. You will be even luckier to see a pine marten, which is extremely rare and lives only in the north of Britain. It is carnivorous, and will even chase and catch squirrels.

Marsh, Pond and Stream

Sometimes ponds and streams are surrounded by marshy areas known as wetlands, where reeds, great willow-herb and purple loosestrife grow. Insects thrive here, and so do the frogs which eat them, and the grass snakes which eat the frogs. Reed-buntings are quite common, and if you are in the east of England you could glimpse a bittern, almost invisible among the stems.

Lake and River

This is where to watch freshwater birds, including swans, geese and ducks. In northern rivers you may see a dipper, bobbing on a rock as it looks for tiny fish and beetles.

Numerous freshwater fishes live in the deep waters of lakes and rivers. The best known are the trout, and the salmon which is really a sea fish that swims upriver each spring to breed in fresh water. Tiny minnows are active and easy to spot, but the large pike is hard to see when it lies still, waiting to ambush its prey.

Small mammals, like water rats and water voles, make burrows in the banks at the water's edge. Larger holes may belong to otters, which are very scarce, especially in the south of Britain.

When the caddis fly is ready to hatch it swims to the surface and climbs free of its case, often up the stem of a plant. It may be caught by the grey wagtail, which hunts near the water.

CADDIS FLY EMERGING

PINTAIL

MUTE SWANS

MOORHEN

MALE MALLARD

FEMALE MALLARD

HIMALAYAN BALSAM

WHITE WATERLILIES

COOT

PIKE

WATER VOLE

Seashore

LESSER BLACK-BACKED GULL

BLACK-HEADED GULL

COMMON STARFISH

LIMPETS

MUSSELS

GREY TOPSHELL

Animals on the seashore live in an ever-changing world. They are covered by the sea when the tide comes in, and left on the shore when it goes out again. Look for them at low tide.

You may find shoals of sand eels close to shore, or buried in wet sand at the sea's edge. Most other animals shelter in rock pools. Any left stranded are eaten by sea birds.

Out of the water, mussels shut their shells tightly, limpets lock onto rocks, and sea anemones become blobs of jelly. When the water covers them, sea anemones spread their tentacles to catch shrimps and tiny fishes.

If you're lucky you may find starfish and hermit crabs. The starfish uses its sucker-like feet to 'walk' over rocks and pull open the mussels and scallops it feeds on. The hermit crab protects its soft body by living in an empty shell, often a whelk-shell, which it swaps for a larger one as it grows.

Sea Cliff and Island

Steep cliffs and rocky islands offer safe breeding places for sea birds. Many of them form large and extremely noisy colonies, resting on ledges that often look too narrow to hold them. Some, like the kittiwakes, build proper nests of mud and seaweed. Others simply lay their eggs on bare rock. The guillemot's eggs are a distinctive pear-shape so that if they are knocked they roll in a circle but don't fall off the ledge. Puffins choose turf-covered rocks or cliffs to dig their nesting burrows – or move into old disused rabbit burrows.

All sea birds live by fishing, and the fulmar, especially, follows fishing boats and feeds on the offal that is thrown overboard when the catch is gutted. The Arctic skua is a 'pirate' who will not only steal a kittiwake's fresh catch, but also bully it in mid-air until it disgorges its last meal.

FULMAR

PUFFINS

HERRING GULL

SEA LAVENDER

CORMORANT

BUCK'S HORN PLANTAIN

Rare and Endangered Species

THE RED SQUIRREL lives high in conifers, pulling cones apart to eat the seeds, though it will forage in oak and beech woods too.

THE OSPREY is a fish-eating hawk. Just a few pairs visit each summer and raise their young near two Scottish lochs.

THE DARTFORD WARBLER is a shy insect-eater that builds its nest in gorse bushes in the south of England. If the winter is cold and long, many die.

THE CHOUGH nests on sea cliffs on the West Coast and in Ireland and hunts inland for insects and spiders.

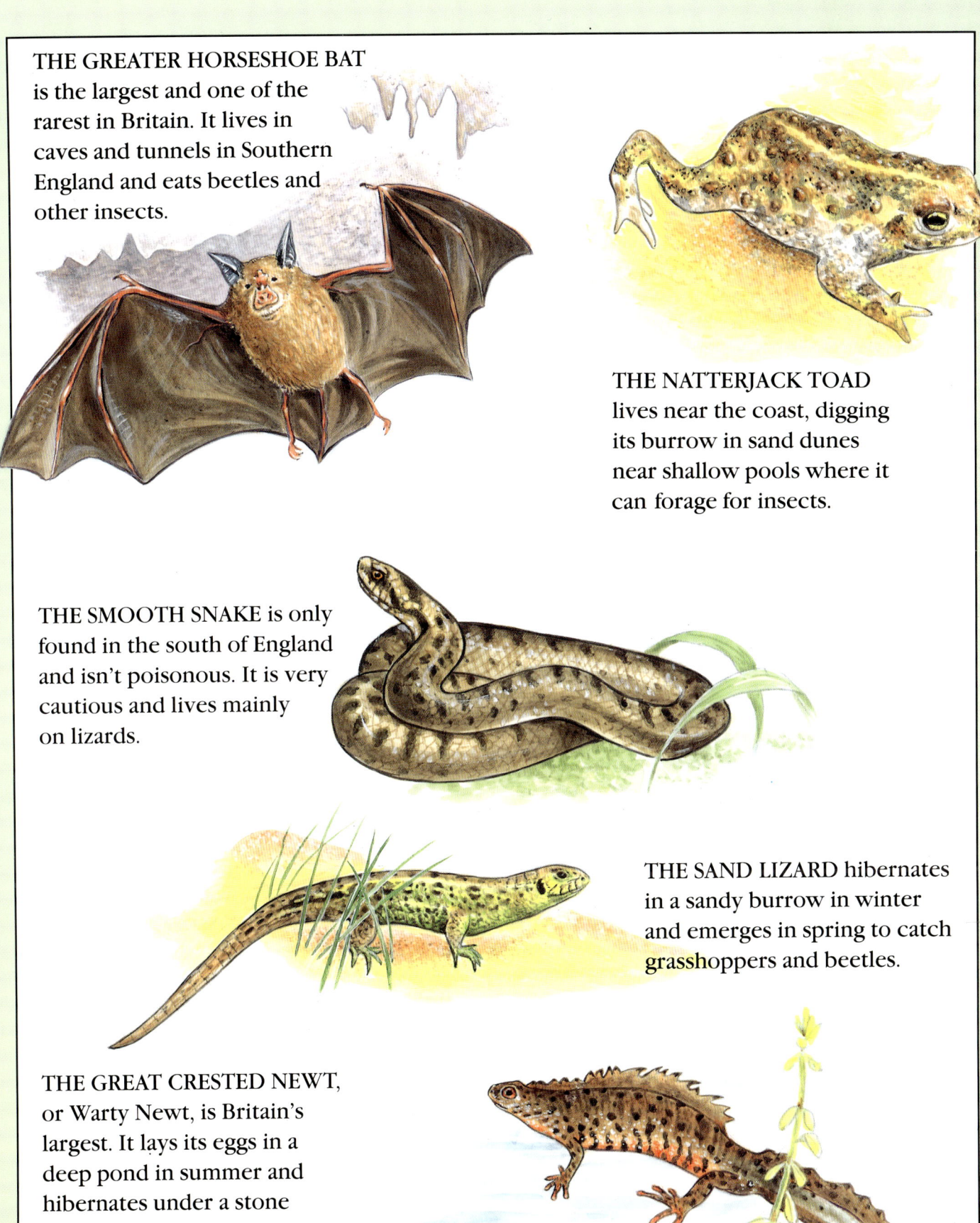

THE GREATER HORSESHOE BAT is the largest and one of the rarest in Britain. It lives in caves and tunnels in Southern England and eats beetles and other insects.

THE NATTERJACK TOAD lives near the coast, digging its burrow in sand dunes near shallow pools where it can forage for insects.

THE SMOOTH SNAKE is only found in the south of England and isn't poisonous. It is very cautious and lives mainly on lizards.

THE SAND LIZARD hibernates in a sandy burrow in winter and emerges in spring to catch grasshoppers and beetles.

THE GREAT CRESTED NEWT, or Warty Newt, is Britain's largest. It lays its eggs in a deep pond in summer and hibernates under a stone in winter.

Tree and Plant Spotter's Guide

The surest way to identify a tree is to look closely at the leaves and the fruit. Never taste the fruit of trees or plants. Some, especially the wild arum, are very poisonous.

Some plants look very different in autumn when fruiting than they do in summer when in flower.

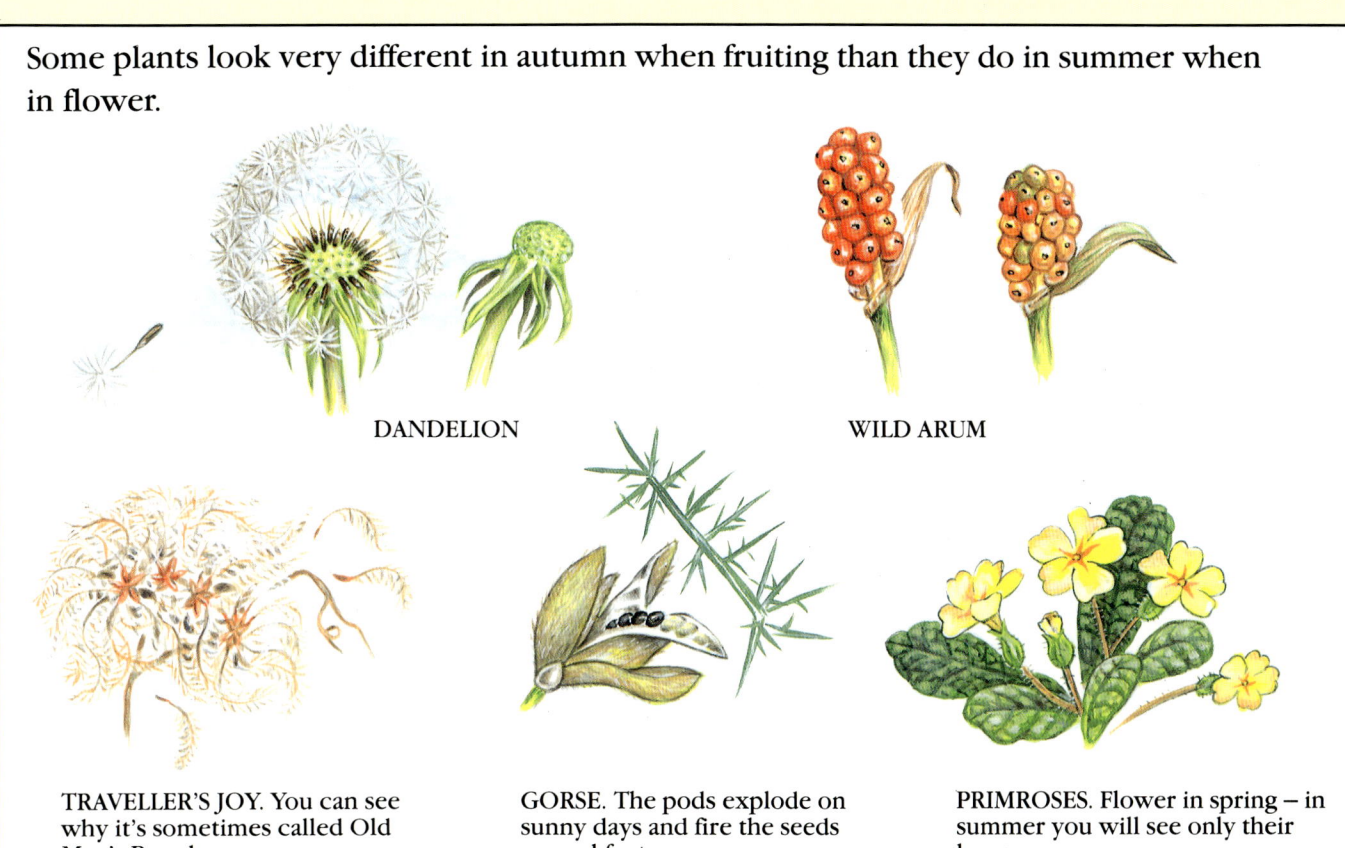

DANDELION

WILD ARUM

TRAVELLER'S JOY. You can see why it's sometimes called Old Man's Beard.

GORSE. The pods explode on sunny days and fire the seeds several feet.

PRIMROSES. Flower in spring – in summer you will see only their leaves.

There are a great many different grasses and rushes in Britain – here is a close-up of the ones in this book.

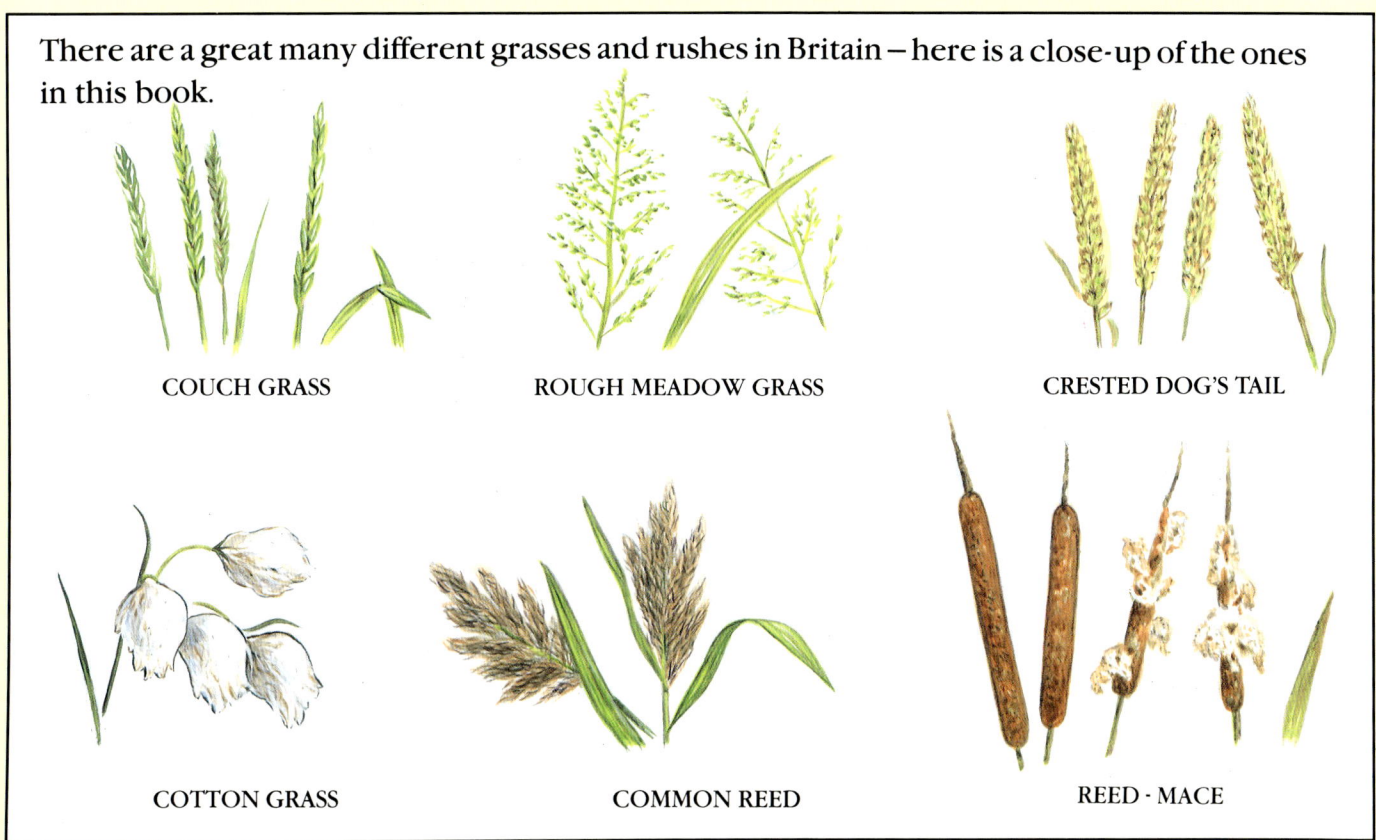

COUCH GRASS

ROUGH MEADOW GRASS

CRESTED DOG'S TAIL

COTTON GRASS

COMMON REED

REED - MACE

Animal and Bird Spotter's Guide

Animals often hide at the approach of humans, but look carefully and you may see signs that will tell you who lives in the area.

There is sheep wool, badger hair and rabbit hair caught on this fence.

This is the skin shed by a grass snake.

This is all that is left of a squirrel's meal.

When a mole is digging a tunnel, it pushes the unwanted earth out at regular intervals.

Footprints are another clue.

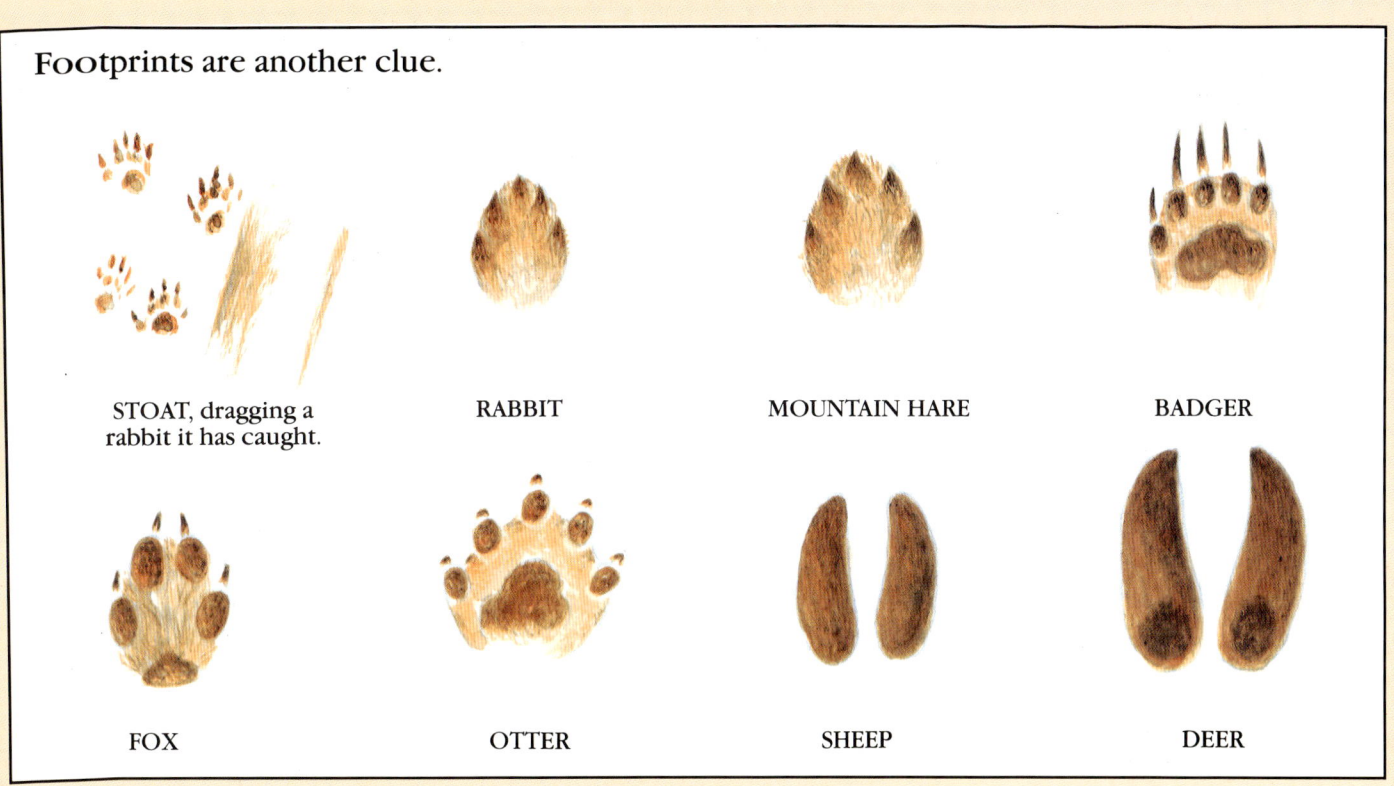

STOAT, dragging a rabbit it has caught.   RABBIT   MOUNTAIN HARE   BADGER

FOX   OTTER   SHEEP   DEER

If you find a bird's nest, never disturb it or touch the eggs.

The lapwing lays her eggs on the ground but their colour makes them hard to see.

The mute swan's egg is the largest laid by any British bird. (113mm x 75mm).

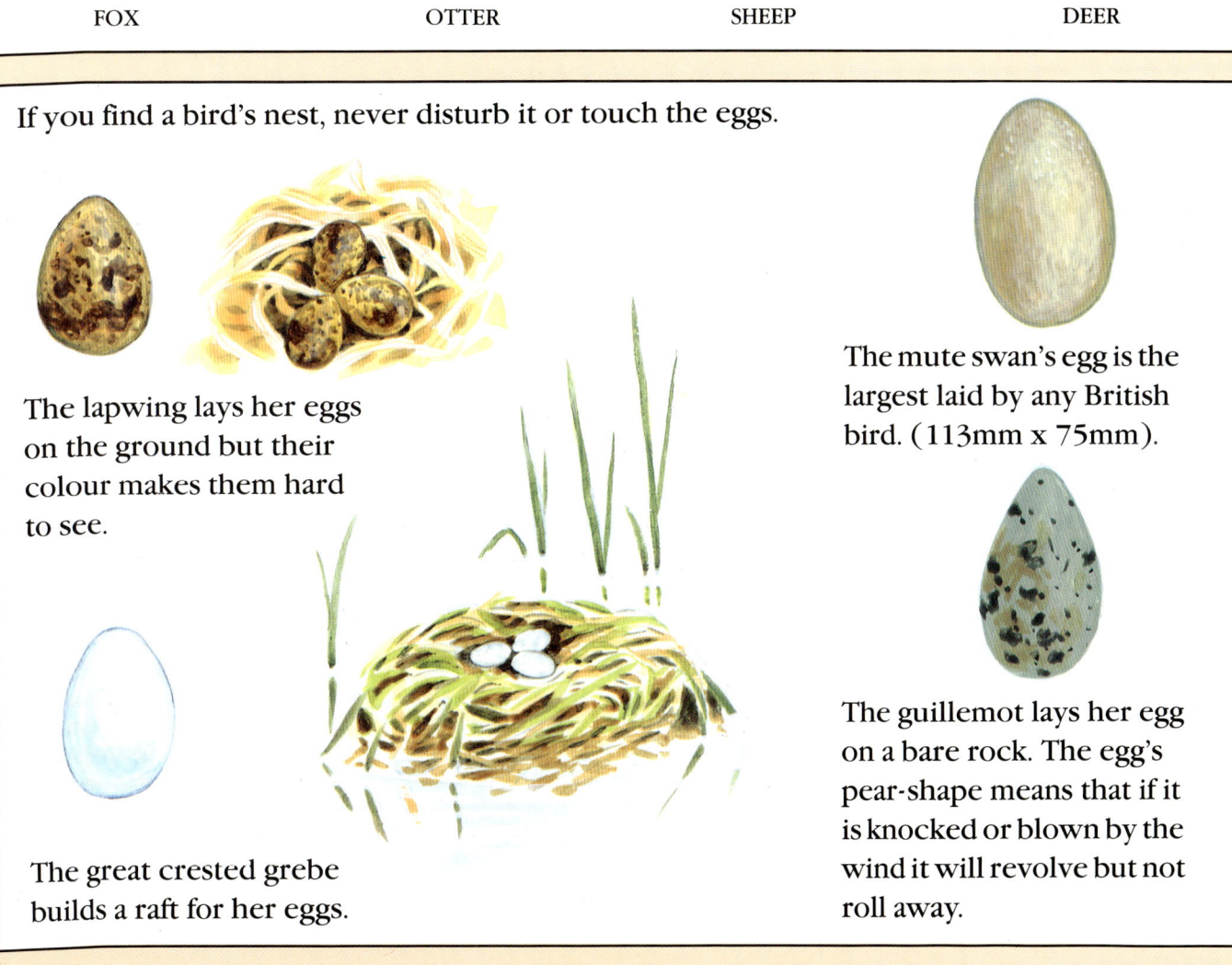

The great crested grebe builds a raft for her eggs.

The guillemot lays her egg on a bare rock. The egg's pear-shape means that if it is knocked or blown by the wind it will revolve but not roll away.

Glossary

Browsing: Feeding on leaves of bushes and trees.
Carnivorous: Flesh-eating.
Conifer: Tree that has cones.
Deciduous: Tree that loses its leaves in winter.
Evergreen: Tree that has green leaves all year.
Hibernate: To sleep through the winter.
Larva: (Larvae, if there is more than one.) Young growing-stage that looks different to its parents, e.g. tadpole or caterpillar.
Mammal: Animal which produces milk to feed its young.